My Special SOMEONE

journal belongs to...

© 2016 Ranch House Press
All rights reserved. Printed in the United States of America.

www.annettebridges.com

ISBN: 978-1-946371-00-3

Journal Prompts

My Special SOMEONE

1. Make a list of all the people who are most special to you? You may want to keep a "My Special Someone" journal for each one of them or dedicate pages to each and "edit" journaling prompts to fit accordingly.
2. What makes you feel loved? What makes your special somebodies feel loved?
3. What can you do with your special somebodies or ask them to do that will allow their unique skills to shine?
4. How do your special somebodies act when they need love, but don't know how to tell you?
5. Is there someone you wish you could tell one more time how much you love them? Write a letter telling them.
6. Is there someone in your life now, whom you need to contact and tell them what they mean to you? What's stopping you?
7. What part of yourself do you guard most closely? Are you able to share it with someone special? Do you think they are able to drop their guard with you?
8. What do you do when you're angry with someone you care about? Do you feel good about your habits for handling anger with your loved one? Why or why not?
9. Describe your relationship with someone special to you. How are you showing one another love? What needs for love are you missing?
10. Write about the first time you held hands with someone special to you.
11. Imagine you have a touch of magic and can make impossible things happen. What would you do for the people most special to you?
12. Make a list of the adjectives that come to mind for your special someone.
13. Make a list of the things someone special does that makes you smile.
14. Describe every detail you can remember to relive the scene of your favorite vacation you've taken with someone special, especially noting how you felt in those moments.
15. Do you have questions you wish someone special to you would answer that you've never asked them?
16. Create a collage from magazine photos that represents someone special to you – their hobbies, their character, what you love about them…
17. Create and describe a memorable moment you can plan for someone special in your life.
18. If you are separated from someone who was special to you, what do you miss the most?
19. When you think of someone special, can you finish this sentence 50 different ways: I love…
20. What are the quotes, sayings and inside jokes you don't ever want to forget that someone special shares with you?
21. Add photographs of you with someone special and caption what you were doing and how you were feeling in those moments.
22. Make a list of the things you admire about the people most special to you.
23. Who are the people in your life that you trust. What qualities do they have they makes you able to trust them?
24. You've been loved in many ways in your life by a variety of people (family, friends, teachers, mentors – even strangers and your pets) who have been special to you. Pen your love biography and list ways you've been loved and by whom.
25. It's sometimes all too easy to hang on to old hurts and grievances we have with those we love most. What retreads of past hurts are you ready to stop rewinding?
26. Think about something that is troubling you about someone special to you. Don't try to solve it – just focus on getting your thoughts out of your head and onto paper.
27. What traits do you hope your loved ones see in you?
28. Describe a new adventure you would like to experience with someone special.
29. Is there anything you feel guilty about, that you hope your loved ones forgive you for?
30. Do you have secret desires that those special to you don't know about that you wish they did?
31. Write letters to those most special to you that would be read after you've passed away.

color your world

ABOUT the CREATOR

Annette Bridges is an author, publisher and women's retreat host on a mission to help every woman realize her story is extraordinary, valuable and noteworthy.

She has published the *Color Your World Journal Series* and formed a journal club to provide community, support and tools for women to record their ideas, feelings, experiences, memories and all the important details of their lives.

Before writing books and publishing journals and coloring books, this former public school and homeschool educator spent a decade writing hundreds of helpful, instructive, and light-hearted columns published by Texas newspapers, parenting magazines, websites and bloggers.

Annette lives on a Texas cattle ranch with her husband John, dachshund Lady and lots of cows. She can drive a tractor but only if wearing a fresh coat of lipstick and it's not her pedicure day!

You can learn more about Annette's books and products, blogs and videos as well as her women's retreats and other events at www.annettebridges.com.

Look for her on social media, too!

MESSAGE from the PUBLISHER

The **Color Your World Journal Series** is a pathway to self-discovery. It's where you write notes to yourself. Be your own cheerleader. Give yourself encouragement. Tell yourself what you're grateful for. Celebrate you!

There are countless reasons to keep a journal including collecting favorite recipes, listing goals and celebrating every experience and every one that's near and dear to you. A journal provides a home for the memories and lessons learned that you never want to forget.

Why a niche journal?

If you're anything like me, you have a journal (or even two or three journals) where you write anything and everything about anything and everything. My challenge comes when trying to find something I've written. I flip and flip through the pages of my two, three or four journals trying to find whatever it is. I never remember which journal I wrote down my whatever's!!

The solution? A niche journal! A journal that has a specific focus and theme! A journal where you can record your ideas, inspirations and things you want to remember in the appropriate journal.

Why big unlined paper?

Because big unlined paper is needed to record big ideas, dreams and memories! You need room to grow, stretch and expand. You need space to think beyond the confines of what you've always done, to pursue new dreams, discover your power and reimagine your purpose again and again. You need pages without lines and limitations to reconnect with your creative, perfectly imperfect self.

Plus, big unlined paper gives you space for more than words. You have plenty of room to doodle, draw or post photographs and clippings, too.

Why color is important?

When you journal, use colored pens and markers! Your world doesn't happen in black and white. Your life should be lived and written about in many colors. Even dark and sad memories feel lighter and brighter when told in color.

Journaling in color affects your mood and perception of your world. Colors evoke calm, cheer and comfort. Using color can lift your spirit and inspire your imagination. You may be surprised by all the beautiful benefits from adding more color into your life story.

When journaling, give yourself time to listen to your heart and reflect. Breathe in the moments. Feel. Be quiet. Let yourself be totally and thoroughly present with your thoughts. Let your heart transform you and teach you new insights. Open your mind to consider new ideas and possibilities. You may find that what your heart teaches will be life changing.

www.ingramcontent.com/pod-product-compliance
Lightning Source LLC
Chambersburg PA
CBHW051253110526
44588CB00025B/2974